Who Am I, Lord?

Who Am I, Lord?

Cindy A. Boatwright

Illustrator Steve Cason

Xulon Press
2301 Lucien Way #415
Maitland, FL 32751
407.339.4217
www.xulonpress.com

© 2021 by Cindy A. Boatwright

Illustrator: Steve Cason

Unless otherwise indicated, Scripture quotations taken from the King James Version
(KJV) – public domain.

Printed in the United States of America.

Paperback ISBN-13: 978-1-66283-758-6
Ebook ISBN-13: 978-1-66283-759-3

Who am I, Lord?
Why do You love me so?

Mommy says if I read the Bible, it will tell me all I need to know.

It tells how You created me
and how I am not a mistake.

It tells how You sent Your Son Jesus
to die on the cross for our sake.

So much love You have for us, God.
I hope I can love You the same.

To be a child of God, I must believe in Jesus's name.

Your Word says I am blessed
and I am chosen and set free!

I am loved and accepted, but I still make mistakes. How can this be?

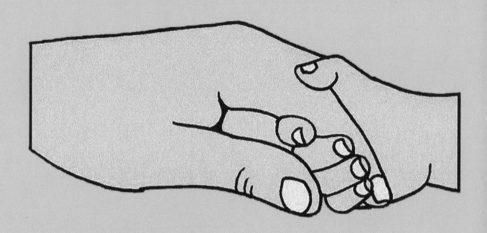

Even though I am Your child, I can't understand all the things You have for me and how You hold my hand.

God, I love you and want You to know I am thankful for Your blessings; each day, my love for You grows.

CPSIA information can be obtained
at www.ICGtesting.com
Printed in the USA
BVHW021418281221
625053BV00022B/1003